Jeff Kinney

CHILDREN'S STORYTELLERS

by Christina Leaf

BLASTOFF! READERS
4

BELLWETHER MEDIA • MINNEAPOLIS, MN

Note to Librarians, Teachers, and Parents:

Blastoff! Readers are carefully developed by literacy experts and combine standards-based content with developmentally appropriate text.

Level 1 provides the most support through repetition of high-frequency words, light text, predictable sentence patterns, and strong visual support.

Level 2 offers early readers a bit more challenge through varied simple sentences, increased text load, and less repetition of high-frequency words.

Level 3 advances early-fluent readers toward fluency through increased text and concept load, less reliance on visuals, longer sentences, and more literary language.

Level 4 builds reading stamina by providing more text per page, increased use of punctuation, greater variation in sentence patterns, and increasingly challenging vocabulary.

Level 5 encourages children to move from "learning to read" to "reading to learn" by providing even more text, varied writing styles, and less familiar topics.

Whichever book is right for your reader, Blastoff! Readers are the perfect books to build confidence and encourage a love of reading that will last a lifetime!

This edition first published in 2016 by Bellwether Media, Inc.

No part of this publication may be reproduced in whole or in part without written permission of the publisher. For information regarding permission, write to Bellwether Media, Inc., Attention: Permissions Department, 5357 Penn Avenue South, Minneapolis, MN 55419.

Library of Congress Cataloging-in-Publication Data

Leaf, Christina.
  Jeff Kinney / by Christina Leaf.
     pages cm. – (Blastoff! Readers: Children's Storytellers)
  Summary: "Simple text and full-color photographs introduce readers to Jeff Kinney. Developed by literacy experts for students in kindergarten through third grade"– Provided by publisher.
  Includes bibliographical references and index.
  Audience: Ages 5-8
  Audience: K to grade 3
  ISBN 978-1-62617-267-8 (hardcover: alk. paper)
  1. Kinney, Jeff–Juvenile literature. 2. Authors, American–21st century–Biography–Juvenile literature. 3. Children's stories–Authorship–Juvenile literature. I. Title.
  PS3611.I634Z74 2016
  813'.6–dc23
  [B]
                                2015000060

Printed in the United States of America, North Mankato, MN.

Table of Contents

Who Is Jeff Kinney?   4

An Ordinary Kid   6

Igdoof and a Wimpy Kid   10

Wimpy No More   14

A Journal, Not a Diary   16

Keeping Kids Laughing   20

Glossary   22

To Learn More   23

Index   24

Who Is Jeff Kinney?

Jeff Kinney is the creator of the wildly popular *Diary of a Wimpy Kid*. This **series** has had great **international** success.

It has won several awards and topped the *New York Times* Best Seller list. The books have made millions of kids excited about reading!

An Ordinary Kid

Jeff was born on February 19, 1971. He grew up in Maryland with his parents and three siblings.

"I would recommend to any kid out there to keep a journal."
Jeff Kinney

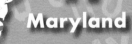

Maryland

N
W   E
S

Greg

Jeff had an ordinary childhood. He fought with siblings and had wimpy moments. Some of these experiences would later **inspire** his writing.

> "If you have a dream let it grow, and maybe one day you will be able to see it fly."
>
> Jeff Kinney

When Jeff was young, he read **comic strips** in the daily newspaper. He also liked to read his dad's collection of old comic books. Jeff enjoyed reading the stories about Donald Duck and Scrooge best.

Jeff loved to doodle. He wanted to create cartoons like the ones he read in the newspaper.

Calvin and Hobbes

The Far Side

fun fact
Some of Jeff's favorite comics were *Calvin and Hobbes* and *The Far Side*.

Igdoof and a Wimpy Kid

When Jeff entered college, he started drawing more seriously. He **submitted** a cartoon called *Igdoof* to his school's newspaper.

"**You might not have a success right out of the gate, but if you keep developing [an idea], you might end up with something really good.**"
Jeff Kinney

Igdoof

Igdoof became a daily strip. After graduation, Jeff tried for several years to sell it to major newspapers, but had no luck.

Meanwhile, Jeff got a job at a web site called FunBrain. He designed educational games for kids. At night, he worked on new cartoons. These were about a wimpy kid named Greg.

In 2004, Jeff showed his cartoons to his boss. The two decided to **publish** some of his comics on FunBrain every day.

Wimpy No More

Comic Con
2006

Thousands of kids were reading Jeff's comic strip online every day. Then, in 2006, Jeff attended **Comic Con** in New York. There, he showed his work to publishers.

SELECTED WORKS

Diary of a Wimpy Kid (2007)
Rodrick Rules (2008)
The Last Straw (2009)
Dog Days (2009)
The Ugly Truth (2010)
Cabin Fever (2011)
The Third Wheel (2012)
Hard Luck (2013)
The Long Haul (2014)
Old School (2015)

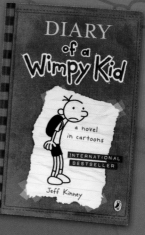

! fun fact

Jeff originally wrote *Diary of a Wimpy Kid* for adults.

One agreed to publish it as a children's book. *Diary of a Wimpy Kid* was given a small first **run**, but copies sold quickly. Jeff's book became a best seller!

A Journal, Not a Diary

Jeff writes his books in a unique way. He makes them look like a kid's journal. Both words and cartoons tell the story.

We were getting our stuff from our lockers at the end of the day, and Rowley came up to me and said—

I have told Rowley at least a billion times that now that we're in middle school, you're supposed to say "hang out," not "play." But no matter how many noogies I give him, he always forgets the next time.

I've been trying to be a lot more careful about my image ever since I got to middle school. But having Rowley aroun[d] ... [h]elping.

18

I met Rowley a few years ago when he move[d] into my neighborhood.

His mom bought him this book called "How t[o] Make Friends in New Places," and he came [to] my house trying all these dumb gimmicks.

I guess I kind of felt sorry for Rowle[y] decided to take him under my wing.

It's been great having him around, mos[t] [...] all the tricks Rodrick p[...]

Greg, the **narrator**, is an average kid trying to survive middle school. He worries about being cool and he fights with his brothers. He also sometimes gets into trouble.

Many kids have similar struggles as Greg. In fact, some stories are based on Jeff's childhood. This helps readers connect with Greg.

Greg does not always do the right thing, but the results are always funny. His hilarious experiences as an unpopular kid have made the books instant favorites.

POP CULTURE CONNECTION

In 2010, the first *Diary of a Wimpy Kid* movie hit theaters. Kids liked seeing the adventures of Greg with real actors. Two other movies followed soon after.

IT'S NOT A DIARY, IT'S A MOVIE.

DIARY of a Wimpy Kid

IN THEATRES MARCH 19

Keeping Kids Laughing

The tenth Wimpy Kid book was published in 2015. Jeff is not done with Greg yet. He plans on writing more Wimpy Kid books and helping with the movies.

"A school library is a place where a kid can escape to a new world or a new point of view."
Jeff Kinney

IMPORTANT DATES

1971: Jeff Kinney is born in Maryland.

1989: *Igdoof* is first published.

1998: Jeff begins working on a book about middle school for adults.

2004: *Diary of a Wimpy Kid* first appears on FunBrain.com.

2006: Jeff brings his book to New York Comic Con.

2007: *Diary of a Wimpy Kid* is published.

2009: Jeff is named one of the world's most influential people by *Time* magazine.

2010: The *Diary of a Wimpy Kid* movie opens.

2012: Jeff is awarded Author of the Year at the Children's Choice Book Awards.

2014: The ninth Wimpy Kid book, *The Long Haul*, is published.

2015: The tenth Wimpy Kid book, *Old School*, is published.

Some day, Jeff wants to make other books, too. He does not know if they will be as successful as the Wimpy Kid series. But he hopes they will keep kids reading and laughing.

Glossary

Comic Con—an event for fans of comics, video games, television, and other forms of pop culture

comic strips—brief series of drawings in panels that are funny or that tell a story

inspire—to give someone an idea about what to do or create

international—in countries other than the United States

narrator—the character who tells a story

publish—to print someone's work for a public audience

run—the number of books printed at one time

series—a number of things that are connected in a certain order

submitted—gave something for approval

To Learn More

AT THE LIBRARY

Gunderson, Megan M. *Jeff Kinney*. Edina, Minn.: ABDO Pub. Co., 2012.

Kinney, Jeff. *Diary of a Wimpy Kid: Greg Heffley's Journal*. New York, N.Y.: Amulet Books, 2007.

Webster, Christine, and Karen Durrie. *Jeff Kinney*. New York, N.Y.: AV2 by Weigl, 2013.

ON THE WEB

Learning more about Jeff Kinney is as easy as 1, 2, 3.

1. Go to www.factsurfer.com.

2. Enter "Jeff Kinney" into the search box.

3. Click the "Surf" button and you will see a list of related web sites.

With factsurfer.com, finding more information is just a click away.

Index

awards, 5
Calvin and Hobbes, 9
childhood, 6, 7, 8, 9, 18
Comic Con, 14
Diary of a Wimpy Kid, 4, 11, 15, 16, 17, 18, 19, 20, 21
Donald Duck, 8
drawing, 9, 10, 17
education, 10, 11
family, 6, 7, 8
Far Side, The, 9
FunBrain, 12, 13
Igdoof, 10, 11
important dates, 21
jobs, 12, 13
Maryland, 6
movies, 19, 20
New York, 14
New York Times, 5
pop culture connection, 19
quotes, 6, 8, 10, 20
sales, 5, 15
Scrooge, 8

selected works, 15
themes, 17, 18, 19
writing, 7, 15, 16, 17, 18, 20, 21